Eugene Nwosu was born in Nigeria in 1958 and now lives in Dublin with his family. He worked in accountancy and management for years before going into private business. His ongoing search for positive living and success was motivated by his own tough childhood. Over fifteen years of studying and practising positive mental attitudes (PMA) have allowed him harness his knowledge and experience to make a positive difference in other people's lives.

CUT YOUR OWN FIREWOOD

The Ultimate Power to Succeed

Eugene Nwosu

To

St Louis Primary School with love and best wishes — [signature]

THE COLLINS PRESS

Published by The Collins Press, Carey's Lane, The Huguenot
Quarter, Cork

Printed in Ireland by Sci Print, Shannon

Jacket design by Upper Case Ltd., Cork

ISBN: 1-898256-36-5

Dedication

Dedicated to my wife, Christine, one of the greatest blessings to my life, whose strong character, hard work, support, sincere criticism, motivation, and love helped make this book possible; to our son, Augustine Operah who is the light, inspiration and source of energy, and bond in our lives; to my late mother, Mrs Hulda Nwosu who passed on very early in my life – before I could walk or utter my first love-word of 'thank you Mum'; to my late father, Mr Gad Nwosu who taught me from an early age to be humble, have faith in the Almighty Creator, and above all, to always believe in myself and my abilities to accomplish anything; to all those, too numerous to mention, who have supported and helped me in my long and incessant struggle for freedom and success, especially my friends Emman and Comfort Enumah, my brothers Theophilus, and Reverend Honest, and sisters Caroline, Joy, Hapinnes, and Faith Nwosu.

To my heroes and role models who provide my inner strength, inspiration, and Ultimate Power – thank you!

Acknowledgements

The weight of my struggles towards success have been made lighter by the support and encouragement of so many people. In particular, my sincere appreciation goes to:

Sri Harold Klemp and his predecessor, the late Paul Twitchell, Spiritual Leaders of Eckankar for their up-lifting and inspiring new-age spiritual teaching. Robert Pye for his spiritual aid.

Niall Wallace, a friend indeed, who has shared some of the burden of my challenges and tribulations.

Ed Parkinson, whose spiritual friendship and love benefited me immensely.

Roddy Peavoy of Impact Design Studio for his editorial contribution.

George Robinson of Impact Design Studio whose artistic talent in typesetting and design has resulted in a unique and reader-friendly format.

My humble thanks to all my friends, former work colleagues, business colleagues and associates, especially A.I. Galadanci, whose friendship and support have helped advance my experience and knowledge in life.

I must not fail to commend the love and charity shown by those who took time out from their usually busy schedule to read the manuscript and send their comments in writing.

May the Blessing be!

Contents

Introduction

You owe it to yourself to recognise now that you have a purpose in life. Within your consciousness lies that *Ultimate Creative Power* to transform your life into your greatest dreams. You are the sole guide of the *Ultimate Creative Power* of your consciousness. Your primary purpose in life must be to harness that natural creative energy, conscientiously draw from it, and regularly apply it positively for the achievement of worthwhile goals.

The quality and level of your success in life – financially, personally, emotionally, and socially – will greatly improve if you positively activate and expand your consciousness. You are the architect of events in your life. Nature has given you special talents, skills and abilities – do not allow negative thinking to block out your right to nature's abundant energy. You can accomplish anything you want if you strongly believe in your ability, and are able to devote a major portion of your time to your goal.

Take charge of your state of consciousness and constantly communicate the positive to yourself – that way you will awaken the resourceful you. Become aware of your exact needs. Stimulate your consciousness regularly with your *Ultimate Desires* and you will become what you programme yourself to be.

You must resolve to focus on what you truly want. Accept your responsibility and turn your life's struggles into potential opportunities. Take worthwhile actions to master your own life, and make positive progress toward your goals and you will overcome fear. Control your fears; turn them into blessings and develop the confident you.

Change your environment by changing your belief system. You possess the same God given *Ultimate Power* of intelligence and reasoning as the most successful person you know. But the difference is that the successful person is able to develop and tap into that *Ultimate Source* regularly and conscientiously.

Stop doubting your abilities and open up your consciousness to fresh ideas and new opportunities. You can change your current circumstances by remodelling your consciousness positively beyond its current parameter. Reactivate your *Ultimate Power of Belief* and restore to yourself that inner confidence and will to excel.

Transform your failures, defeats, and adversities into a wealth of experience, knowledge and intelligence to become triumphant. You must know where you want to go and set out plans for getting there. Condition your consciousness to believe in great success and you will achieve wonderful things.

Everything and everybody is part of the *Ultimate Whole* – everything forms part of the invisible atom of the *Ultimate Creator*. The world is full of lovely things. Fill your consciousness with love and let it overflow. You need to harness and apply your talent and resources positively for the betterment and love of mankind.

This book will give you the powerful tools you need to reactivate, uplift and expand the *Ultimate Power* of your creative consciousness to achieve financial and personal success and happiness. You will learn how to positively utilise the *Ultimate Power* of your *will* to regain control of your life. You will be able to harness the *Ultimate Power* of your creative consciousness and use it to serve your needs – to become *rich, content, and happy!*

My Humble Prayer

I declare myself a vehicle to the
Almighty Creator.

I declare myself a vehicle to the
Ultimate Power of my Creative Consciousness and
Divine Intelligence.

I will give my Best to Life

So I will receive the Best from Life.

May the Blessings of the
Almighty Creator Be.

EUGENE NWOSU

What is in this Book for You

The universal truth in this book you already possess – your consciousness was blest from birth with the *Ultimate Power* to reason, know, choose, and believe. This book will help you activate, ignite, and expand the *Ultimate Power* of your creative consciouness to achieve great and worthwhile success in your life.

This book is an education in the universal truth and positive way of life. It is recommended that it be used as a one year foundation discourse on human development.

Practise reading this book in a non-noisy, and private environment of your own – away from anybody, until you develop the *Ultimate Power of Confidence* necessary for the achievement of your set goals. You should study a chapter per month. For all intents and purposes, feel free to read through all the chapters in quick succession. But, for greater benefit, study one chapter per month. Read a page or two first thing in the morning at home or in the office, and last thing before you sleep at night. Sit quietly, with eyes closed, and contemplate for about ten to twenty minutes. This way, you will implant the essential ingredients of the *Ultimate Power* into your creative consciousness for great and wonderful achievements.

At the end of each chapter you will find an exercise note to record your *Triumphs* and *Challenges*. *Triumphs* would be what you achieved within the course of each chapter, and *Challenges* would be what you plan and hope to achieve. Be specific. Give dates, names, and details of achieved and/or expected results. Keeping such records will uplift your consciousness to greater heights. Utilise your personal notebook to elaborate in writing your progress, successes and challenges and you will expand the *Ultimate Power of your creative consciousness* to achieve worthwhile goals ... *Go for it!*

Chapter 1

Make that Change Right Now

Your consciousness, through natural creation, has been entrusted with highly potent and pure energy, and you possess the natural ability to do whatever it takes to succeed.

Your idea of true success could be to win the respect of intelligent people, to be financially comfortable, to reach the top of your career, to gain the affection of children, to laugh often and much, to appreciate beauty, to find the best in other people, to earn the appreciation of sincere critics, to have the wisdom to endure the betrayal of false friends, to leave this world a little better – whether by healthy offspring, a garden patch, an emancipated social condition, or to ensure that another has breathed easier because you have lived.

> *Your consciousness has no limitation. The only limitations there are have been created by your thinking process. Reactivate that fire in your consciousness now – and constantly refuel it with only the positive.*

No one drifts to success. Your consciousness has no limitation. The only limitations there are have been created by your thinking process. Reactivate that fire in your consciousness now – and constantly refuel it with only the positive.

You have a purpose in life. Start now to make plans

for the achievement of those burning desires. Start now to set out in clear terms the plans. You must at this moment *decide exactly what your goal is and lay out the steps by which you intend to reach it.*

You will attract all the opportunities that you deserve if you *act with clear purpose and plan.* You will get all that you need – but you must first *know what you want and define it.*

Decide your goals, set out your plans, be committed to them, and you will find the help you need to succeed. With definite purpose, you will overcome the defeat and adversities that will stand in your way to success. You must *maintain strong belief in yourself, in what you are doing, and what you want to do;* and no adversity will be too difficult to overcome.

Stop drifting, and make today the day you start achieving.

The Ultimate Power to change

The road to success is a progressive path. It must always be under construction. Within your consciousness lies the power to magically transform your life according to your greatest dreams. There are many wondrous success stories around you. Success is achieved daily. Success is no longer the reserve of aristocratic inheritance. Opportunities abound everywhere for anyone with imagination and vision – positive and expanded consciousness to achieve success beyond expectation.

> *Opportunities abound everywhere for anyone with imagination and vision – positive and expanded consciousness to achieve success beyond expectation.*

Open up your consciousness now to positively shape your perceptions, or someone else will shape them for you. You do not need to respond to someone else's plan for you. Within your consciousness lies the ability and *Ultimate Power* to produce the results you desire most, and in the process create value for others.

You must seize that *Ultimate Power* to direct your own personal kingdom, your own thought process and the behaviour to produce the precise results you desire. *Your ability to define your needs and the needs of the people you care about, and to achieve them, is Ultimate Power.*

> *Your ability to define your needs and the needs of the people you care about, and to achieve them, is Ultimate Power.*

Your consciousness contains the golden key to magical and *Ultimate Power*. You should harness and use it now to succeed.

The Ultimate action to change

Incredible successes have all been preceded by action. Action is what produces results. Knowledge is raw, magical power when in the hands of anyone who can utilise it through effective action.

> *Learn how to live your own life.*

Power is the ability to act. You must decide upon your definite goal. Write it down, and commit it to memory. You should decide exactly how you plan to achieve it. Begin putting your plan into action immediately.

You must decide now on what to make your future. Your future will become what you make it to be. You are the sole guidance of your consciousness. You have an unchallengeable prerogative over your consciousness. The Almighty Creator gave every living creature that prerogative.

Wake up your genius by simply directing your consciousness toward objectives of your choosing – without permitting outside influences to discourage or mislead you. Learn how to live your own life. One of the wonderful rewards of success is self-satisfaction. Resolve to cut your own firewood and it will warm you twice.

> *Nothing is impossible for the one who believes in the possible.*

That satisfaction of knowing you have done a job and done it well – that you have achieved the goal you set for yourself – is the mark of true success. Constantly motivate yourself to achieve success. Develop that burning desire for something that you wish to have in order to reach a greater goal you have set for yourself.

Merely wishing for something will not produce the desired result. Burning desire fuelled by definite decision will produce a successful result. Once you possess that burning desire, you will develop an intensity of purpose that will allow you to simply brush aside seemingly insurmountable obstacles. Nothing is impossible for the one who believes in the possible.

You must set yourself definite goals in life. Direct your thoughts and commit all your energies to realising them. You must not allow momentary setbacks throw you off-course. You will find an equivalent benefit from every adversity which can help you get back on track to attaining your goal.

No mountain will be high enough to stop the person who is determined to reach a life goal. Determine to attain success today. Start from wherever you stand at this very moment – make the best of whatever tools you may have and continue to acquire whatever else you may need along the way.

Your purpose is to realise your potential. You are given life and your purpose should be to make a success of it. You can measure your success by comparing what you are actually achieving with what you are capable of achieving.

The potential power of your consciousness will remain untapped and idle until you discover what it is you want. Break that barrier which had been created by self-imposed limitations on your consciousness and which prevents you from making a success of your life. You must recognise the uniqueness of your consciousness. Recognising the fact that you are unique is important to the process of awakening your consciousness to definite actions leading to success.

> *No mountain will be high enough to stop the person who is determined to reach a life goal.*

Communicate to change

Communication is potential power. What you do in life is, to a great extent, determined by how you communicate with yourself. What you say to yourself and how you picture yourself determines how much you value yourself.

The magical power which extraordinarily successful people have over the average person is their incredible ability to get themselves to take action. You can develop this wonderful magic. The gift is within your consciousness. Those who have mastered the magic power of communication can change their experience of the world and the world's experience of them.

The level of your success in life – financially, personally, emotionally, and socially – will be improved if you expand your consciousness. Communicate the positive to your consciousness and you will achieve internal bliss, joy, ecstasy, love and happiness.

> *How you feel is not as the result of what is happening in your life – it is the interpretation of what is happening.*

The quality of your life is determined not by what happens to you, but rather by what you do about what happens. How you feel is not as the result of what is happening in your life – it is the interpretation of what is happening. Decide now to feel only the positive. Begin now to act positively. Choose now to perceive only the positive in your life – for nothing has any meaning besides the meaning you give it.

Realise that you are already producing results in your life. They may not yet be the results you desire. You will be able to control your consciousness, your activities and general behaviour to a degree you never believed possible. You will turn up the light and sound of the positive messages in your consciousness, you will dim the pictures and block out the sound of negative ones.

Every disciplined effort you make will bring with it multiple rewards. Follow a consistent path to success. Every success story follows a consistent path of excellence. Interpret the positive to your consciousness. Communicate the positive to your consciousness – *make that change right now!*

The genius you

The ability to perform at exceptional levels in at least one area of your life is within you. You can discover the genius you through an expansion of your consciousness. Stimulate your consciousness through positive contemplation, reading of positive and goal orientated materials. The extent of your successes and achievements will depend on how far you can stimulate your consciousness. The degree to which you stimulate and develop your consciousness determines your achievements in life. You are the architect of events in your life.

> *The degree to which you stimulate and develop your consciousness determines your achievements in life.*

Success and failures will be yours for the asking. You are reading this book because you want the *Ultimate Power* to achieve the successes you deserve in life. Therefore, in the course of this book, the use of the words 'failure' and 'negative' will be limited.

Everybody is born with unique, highly potent genius quality.

Opportunity does knock more than once – numerous times – in fact every day of your life. There is no limit to chance. Each new day brings a new beginning. You must understand this and seize the initiative now. There are fresh and wonderful opportunities throughout our lives. We only have to look around us to discover the abundance of opportunities.

> *You are the architect of events in your life.*

Don't wait for opportunity to come to you – go and find it. Find the right opportunity for you and it will turn your ordinary circumstances to wonderful and exceptional circumstances. Stop doubting yourself and the world around you.

With an expanded consciousness and positive outlook you will start to recognise the unlimited opportunity that lies around you. Look to the present and future. Learn to see abundance where others may see scarcity. Many successes revolve around opportunities achieved following a crisis, adversity or failure. Your failure will open up new opportunities thereby providing a springboard to success.

Nothing rings a bell to your consciousness like failure. The very bright and clear stop sign is held up to your consciousness by failure – making you stop and assess your life and look for opportunities. The more you fail the better your chance of success in future.

There are unlimited opportunities there for you – regardless of your ambition, profession, or current occupation. You have the *Ultimate Power* to create the ideas and opportunities to make you rich and successful in every area of your life.

> *Learn to see abundance where others may see scarcity.*

Expand your boundaries, expand your consciousness and grasp nature's magic around you. Tap the ocean of love and mercy with boldness and seize the opportunities. You are a *born genius*. Harness and utilise the *genius you* now to achieve great and wonderful things in your life.

The Ultimate Formula

● Determine exactly what you want. Your unique ability to reason for yourself sets you apart from other forms of life. You must cultivate passion – a reason; a consuming, energising, obsessive purpose to succeed. Once you develop that passion to achieve greatness – wonderful things will start to happen to you.

● Take action toward the achievement of your desires. You have the capacity to achieve great things. Your potential is there and waiting to be used. There are no limitations on your potential for success.

● Believe that you will get what your consciousness desires. Your belief about what you are and what you can be will greatly determine what you will be. Believe in magic and you will live a magical life.

● You must organise your resources. Having the resources is not enough – you must use those resources in the most effective way.

● Formulate your strategy. You can do virtually anything if you can apply your resources to take effective action.

● Be committed to change and being flexible until you create the life you desire.

● Have a clear understanding and sense of who you are and why you do what you do. Values are specific belief systems you have about what is right and wrong for you.

● Communicate the positive to your consciousness. Take any challenge that life gives you and communicate that experience to your consciousness in a positive way that will cause you to change things.

Make that Change Right Now

Triumph Notes

PROGRESS • ACHIEVEMENT • SUCeSS

Cut Your Own Firewood

Challenge Notes
PLANS • TARGETS • HOPES

Chapter **2**

Start Growing Again

There are wondrous opportunities around you, and one thing you do not have enough of is time. Become a warrior. Be obsessive about success. Make the most of what you have and you will achieve ultimate success. The combination of your physical and intellectual energy will propel you to take opportunities and shape them.

You have in you an abundant reserve of strength, imagination, vision, insight and creativity. If you feel inadequate in a particular area this is because you have imposed limitations on yourself. Nature has given you special talents, skills and abilities. Do not allow negative thinking to block out your right to nature's abundant energy. Exercise your *Ultimate Power* of choice now. Go to nature's ocean of love and mercy within you, with large buckets and not with tea cups.

> *Do not allow negative thinking to block out your right to nature's abundant energy.*

Whatever you ask and strongly believe, nature will certainly bestow upon you. Think and believe big, and so it shall be given unto you. Think magic and you will radiate magic, and magical things will begin to happen to you.

Success is no accident. Start now to expand your consciousness. Only by an expansion of your consciousness will you discover the unique you. Everybody and everything is created for a purpose. You owe a duty to yourself to discover what unique talent you possess and the contribution you can make in this lifetime.

Your Ultimate Power of choice

Your growth and success will begin the moment you understand that life is about your choice to grow. It is about using your *Ultimate Power* of choice to acquire the knowledge and skills you need to live more fully and effectively. Realise the fact that life is meant to be a never-ending education. Make your life the adventure that it's meant to be. Choose to make your life a journey of discovery, an exploration into your potential. Experience the joy and exuberance in your willingness to risk, your openness to change and your ability to create what you want for your life.

> *Choose to make your life a journey of discovery, an exploration into your potential.*

Choose now to recognise your *Ultimate Power* as an individual – that anything you set your consciousness to work on will become a reality. Choose to make your thoughts your own – to keep, change, share and contemplate. Your freedom of choice is your *Ultimate Power*. The freedom to think whatever you choose to allow into your consciousness is your *Ultimate Power*.

> *Experience the joy and exuberance in your willingness to risk, your openness to change, and your ability to create what you want for your life.*

Control your thoughts. Determine your feelings and choose how you respond or act in any given situation. You should no longer blame circumstances for any situation you may find yourself in. Start right now to examine your life in the light of choices you have made, or failed to make – that way you will begin to see that you are the person responsible for how you feel. Accept that you are the sum total of your choices made to date and, therefore, with new choices you can decide to be, have, or do anything you want for future success.

Stop blaming your circumstances for what you are. Get up and look for the circumstances you want, and if you can't find them, make them. Use your *Ultimate Power* of choice to make positive decisions for your future success. Work repeatedly on your *Ultimate Power* of belief, not simply trying it once, and do not use your initial inability as an excuse to give up.

Recognise the fact that nature determines the results of your choices. You cannot cheat nature and its universal principles. You may have the freedom in your choice of action, but you do not have the choice of the consequences. There are universal principles of cause and effect whereby thoughts are causes and conditions are effects. You can make a choice of results or consequences by making the right choices of action and attitudes. The good that comes to you must be paid for in advance. Usually the bad choices you made are paid for at a later stage.

> *Trying to cheat your way through life will always fail to provide you with the Ultimate Power of success.*

Do not expect to have your cake and eat it. You must not expect to reap what you did not sow. You will experience frustration by wanting both pleasures and prestige of one choice and the consequences of another. Do not blame bad luck, fate or someone else if you waste your life trying to beat the system. Trying to cheat your way through life will always fail to provide you with the *Ultimate Power* of success. You can maintain your *Ultimate Power* of control by choosing again if the original outcome is not to your liking. If you make the right choice, you will get the right outcome; but if you happen to make the wrong choice, you have the *Ultimate*

Power of choice to choose again. The choices you make must be yours. Have complete faith in your consciousness which is your inner guidance and you will develop the *Ultimate Power* of choice.

Improve your circumstances by making better choices now. The decisions you make, your attitude, and the habits you cultivate will create your own physical, emotional and spiritual consciousness. The exercise of your *Ultimate Power* and privilege of free choice will enable you to share all life's opportunities.

You possess much more *Ultimate Power* than you choose to believe. It is absolutely imperative that you recognise the fact that you can choose – you must realise this *Ultimate Power* and choose to be successful now. Do not be a spectator to life's wonderful opportunities. Better to attempt great things, even if sometimes you fail, than to stand on the side-lines of life. Utilise your *Ultimate Power of choice and start growing again!*

> **Do not be a spectator to life's wonderful opportunities.**

The Ultimate Power of desire

You must know precisely what your ultimate desires are. You have in your consciousness an in-built desire to succeed. Get away from ordinary and uneventful existence, and begin now to make your mark in history.

You can accomplish anything you want if you strongly believe in your ability, and devote a major portion of your time to developing it. Over 90 per cent of successful people are self-made. Most billionaires or million-aires were ordinary people who set out to achieve extraordinary results.

Once you know what your heart desires the doors of opportunity will begin to open up to you.

Transform your hopes and wishes into burning desire. Merely wishing will not bring you success. Become a child again and explore your inner-most desires. Once you know what your heart desires, the doors of opportunity will begin to open up to you. Let your desires be the ultimate motivating power. Expand your consciousness and become more receptive to your inner desires, no matter how unachievable or how fantastic they may seem to be at first. Define your desires. Be specific. Write them down, carry them with you twenty-four hours a day. Commit them to your consciousness. Make them a consuming obsession.

The Ultimate Power of belief

You want the best in this lifetime. Believe, and truly believe you can succeed, and you will. Do not confuse belief with wishful thinking. You can move a mountain with your absolute and unquestionable belief. Your consciousness will lead you to ways and means of reaching your goal if you have absolute belief in the *Ultimate Power* of your consciousness.

> *You can move a mountain with your absolute and unquestionable belief.*

Your strong belief will trigger the *Ultimate Power* of your consciousness to create possibilities of success. Your honest and sincere belief that you can succeed will launch you to extraordinary success. Expand your consciousness now. Start believing big and you will begin to grow big. Believe in victory and you will win. You are the sum total of your consciousness. Believe yourself and others will start to believe in you. Good things will start to happen to you once you start to believe in yourself. Your consciousness is blest with an abundance of success potential waiting to be harnessed. Give your consciousness the positive command. Propel yourself to wonderful success by believing you are a success.

> *Expand your consciousness now. Start believing big and you will begin to grow big. Believe in victory and you will win.*

Develop success habits. Train yourself to achieve bigger and more wonderful success. Make the most of yourself and achieve the satisfaction of knowing you are on the road to achievement. Believe you are a success. When faced with a difficult situation, believe you will win. When you compete with someone else, believe you are equal to the best. When opportunity appears, believe you can grasp it. Condition your consciousness to create plans that will produce success.

Recognise the fact that you are better than you may have thought. There is no mystery about success. You do not need to be super-intelligent to achieve success. All you need is to develop that *Ultimate Power* of belief in yourself and your right to succeed. Successful people are not super-humans. Success is achieved through positive nurturing and self-development. Whatever you do, never sell yourself short. Believe in wonderful things. Your belief will bring you great and wonderful success. Believe in the *Ultimate Power* of your creative consciousness to succeed.

> *Believe you are a success. When faced with a difficult situation, believe you will win. When you compete with someone else, believe you are equal to the best. When opportunity appears, believe you can do it.*

The Ultimate resources to grow

You are who you think and believe you are. Your consciousness possesses the ultimate resources to achieve wonderful things. Tap into your inner resources to achieve confidence, love, joy, ecstasy, and inner bliss. Your behaviour at any given moment is the result of the state you are in. Take charge of your state of consciousness and thus your behaviour. Put yourself in an empowering, resourceful state with the *Ultimate Power* of action. However terrible a situation may seem, you can utilise it in a positive and resourceful way to empower yourself. Successful people are able to tap into their most resourceful states on a consistent basis. Nothing is inherently good or bad. You can positively empower yourself in all circumstances. The *Ultimate Power* of success is to perceive things in a way that puts you in such a resourceful state that you are empowered to take the types of quality actions that create your desired outcome. When you perceive that things will work, you create the internal resources you need to produce the state that will support you in producing positive results.

> *Put yourself in an empowering, resourceful state with the Ultimate Power of action.*

> *When you perceive that things will work, you create the internal resources you need to produce the state that will support you in producing positive results.*

Your behaviour is the result of the state of your consciousness; which is the result of your perception; both of which you can change at any given moment. Constantly communicate the positive to yourself and awaken the resourceful you. There is no power like the *Ultimate Power* of resourcefulness. Your behaviour is the result of the state you are in. You must realise that success is a journey – it is the sum total of your attitudes and habits acquired on that journey. You must learn how to put your talents and abilities to use.

You must continuously decide and set new goals and objectives. You must set new and higher goals; for if you don't, you will no longer be successful. You may have been a success in the past, perhaps a great one, but if you no longer set fresh goals and objectives you will cease to be successful. The development of your untapped potential is a worthwhile goal. Start now to do those things which you have not yet done and enjoy the rewards of success, such as recognition, prestige, security, and peace of mind.

> *You must set new and higher goals; for if you don't, you will no longer be successful.*

Wealth, in terms of financial prosperity, when rightfully gained is a measure of success and must be appreciated. Proven past experiences have shown that success is more than just the accumulation of wealth. By contrast no one can be a complete failure no matter how lean their pocket as long as they live a life of daily progress towards goals and service to others. Utilise your *Ultimate Power* to harness and apply your *ultimate resources to start growing again!*

> *Success is more than just the accumulation of wealth. By contrast no one can be a complete failure no matter how lean their pocket as long as they live a life of daily progress towards goals and service to others.*

The Ultimate Formula

- Know exactly what you want. Develop plans for getting what you desire. Strongly believe in your ability to achieve your set goal, and devote a major part of your time to your set goals.

- Become like a master salesperson and learn the art of influencing others to co-operate in a friendly manner to assist you in your plans and purposes.

- Think before you speak. Weigh your words carefully. Express the positive about other people. If you cannot say something positive about someone, do not say anything at all. Express your opinions only after having informed yourself so you can do so intelligently.

- You must budget your time, income and expenditure. Live within your means.

- You must show a keen interest in people, especially those with whom you have something in common, and cultivate a bond of friendship with them.

- You should be open-minded and tolerant on all subjects, and towards all people.

- You should keep abreast of the times and make it an important responsibility to know what is going on, not only in your own business, profession, or community, but throughout the entire world.

- You must keep your consciousness and outlook on life positive at all times. Remember that the space you occupy in the world and the success you enjoy will depend on the quality and quantity of service you render. Make it a habit to render more service than you promised.

- Maintain a keen respect for the Almighty Creator. Devote at least 30 minutes each day to prayer or spiritual contemplation.

- Be helpful to others.

Start Growing Again

Triumph Notes
PROGRESS • ACHIEVEMENT • SUCCESS

Challenge Notes

PLANS • TARGETS • HOPES

Chapter 3

Stretch Your Consciousness Now

Your development will be determined by your thinking. Whether you are consciously aware of it or not, your personal philosophy of life, your way of seeing the world, and your point of view has evolved over the years. Your decisions direct your actions and mould your behaviour – the final product of which is the circumstances and conditions in which you find yourself.

> *Begin to accept responsibility for your life. Stop blaming all your misfortune on the past and present rulers of the society in which you live; for that will distract you from facing the responsibility to act on your own freely, sensibly, and decisively.*

Stretch your consciousness, begin to accept responsibility for your life. Stop blaming all your misfortune on the past and present rulers of the society in which you live, for that will distract you from facing the responsibility to act on your own freely, sensibly, and decisively. Look at the past as history. Look towards the future, for it holds myriad possibilities. No matter where you find yourself at this moment, you can begin to stretch your consciousness and stimulate the ultimate sense of hope and positive anticipation about your future.

You must start to clarify and envisage what you truly want for your life. Stimulate your consciousness regularly with pictures of your ultimate desires. You will become what you think about. You are the product of your imagination. All that you are is as the result of what you have thought. Your life is what your thoughts make it. You will become what you programme your consciousness to be. You shall reap what you sow – your consciousness will nourish whatever you plant.

> *Stimulate your consciousness regularly with pictures of your ultimate desires.*

'To him who has, shall more be given and to him who has not, even that which he has may be taken away', goes a wise and popular saying. Decide now to discover your unique purpose, your areas of excellence, and your consciousness will provide you with the insight, vision, energy, enthusiasm, courage and discipline to break the barrier that may stand in your way to attaining your goals. Start now to realise that you possess within your consciousness unique talents that you need to discover, use and share.

> *Your consciousness will nourish whatever you plant.*

The unique talent with which you are born must be claimed, developed and used. Exploit your unique talent, no matter what, and it shall increase. Share your unique talents and they will multiply. That which you withhold will diminish. Explore the *Ultimate Powers* of your consciousness and achieve extraordinary success.

The Ultimate Power to determine your potential

Nature has compelled you to struggle in order to develop, expand and progress. Success will be unthinkable and even impossible without struggle. The education you receive from the struggles you face is the culmination of the experience you encountered along the way. Education is not necessarily academic education. You can be highly skilled and educated within your field and your environment; as a carpenter, bricklayer, trader and business person, office worker, company executive, driver, salesman, college student, lecturer or teacher, journalist or writer. Academic knowledge is far removed from experience and knowledge acquired through struggle.

Get rid of poverty mentality and watch yourself grow to extraordinary success.

Change your attitude right now and you will begin to create wonderful opportunities. Transform your consciousness with rich and successful desires. Knock and the door of success will open. Ask and strongly believe, and it shall be given to you. Get rid of poverty mentality and watch yourself grow to extraordinary success. Feed your consciousness with positives rather than negatives. Practise positive attitude at home and at work.

Get into the habit of saying – 'I am a success' – to yourself in the morning, afternoon, and just before you go to bed. Repeat 'I am a success' to yourself seven times, each time, until it becomes part and parcel of your consciousness. Start by practising this exercise slowly, in private, taking about three deep breaths at intervals. Make sure you are in a relaxed position. Listen to the sound in your head. You can practise this silently while travelling on the bus, walking, or driving. Your consciousness will absorb this powerful message and lead you to discover the incredible opportunities around you.

The affirmation of success to your consciousness will greatly improve your attitude – a positive attitude that will bring you unexpected opportunities. Keep your mind on what you want and not what you don't want because attitudes are habits of thoughts which can quickly translate into riches or poverty.

Keep your mind on what you want and not what you don't want because attitudes are habits of thoughts which can quickly translate into riches or poverty.

Your struggle will toughen your consciousness to a greater height. You must turn your struggle into opportunities through positive attitudes. Your worthwhile success will come through life in one way or another. Don't run away from struggle. Rather embrace struggle and you will grow and succeed. You possess the *Ultimate Power* to determine your potential. Accept your responsibility and discover the *Ultimate Power* to face your struggle – *determine your potential now* and you will achieve great and wonderful success.

Your worthwhile success will come through life in one way or another. Don't run away from struggle. Rather embrace struggle and you will grow and succeed.

The Ultimate Power to be true to yourself

Start now to be responsible and you will master your own life. Start being in control again, and enjoy the bliss of mastering your life, of being in control. Identify your goals and the price tag. Everything has a price. The price for success is payable in advance, so it is essential to identify and pay the price. There will be sacrifices along the way to success. The sacrifices may come in the form of foregoing pleasure time to study new skills, or tightening the belt while saving for something. Be prepared to pay the price for success.

Sincerity of purpose will propel you to great achievements. Your chances of attaining that wonderful goal will be greatly improved if you have a sincere wish to provide others with a better product or service.

Compare the cost to the wonderful benefits you will receive from achieving your goal and you will see just how small the price is. Remember that everything along the way counts. There is no such thing as a free lunch. You will be responsible for all your actions. Anything you do, or don't do, will enhance your prospect or deter you. You cannot cheat your consciousness. Believe, sincerely believe in your consciousness and your abilities. Sincerity of purpose will propel you to great achievements. Your chances of attaining that wonderful goal will be greatly improved if you have a sincere wish to provide others with a better product or service.

Be sincere and enjoy the ultimate reward of self-satisfaction, self-respect and the spiritual power to live with yourself twenty-four hours a day. Conduct your life sincerely with due regard to that 'invisible *Ultimate*

Power' which can guide you to glory, fame and riches. Others have the right to question your sincerity before they can grant you their time, energy, or money. You can test your sincerity to yourself by making sure you are giving value in service or goods for the profit or wages you hope to make. Do not hope to get something for nothing. You will find it hard to prove your sincerity, but remain true to yourself and the door to the palace of opportunities will open to you. You will achieve your own goals in life by providing others with true and fair value in goods or services rendered. Make the most of yourself and achieve great goals.

> *Remain true to yourself and the door to the palace of opportunities will open to you.*

The Ultimate Power to overcome your fears

Hopefulness will help cure your fears. Erase your fears with your imagination, dreams of hope for a better world, a better life, a better tomorrow. Hope will help you decide your definite goal in life and enable you to translate it into actuality. The feeling of hope and faith that nothing is impossible will enable you to take that important first step.

Avoid procrastination as it would only lead to more doubt and fear. Make the positive step towards your goals and you will overcome fear.

One of the obstacles to success is fear. You must not allow fear to rule your decisions. You must be willing to take risks. The successful person is one who is willing to take risks when sound logic shows they are necessary. Turn your fears into a blessing. Use your fear only as a sign-post to pause and assess a situation before making a decision or taking action. Control your fear and do not allow it to control you. Utilise your *Ultimate Power* of reasoning to turn your fears into a logical reasoning sign-post.

Action as opposed to procrastination will help you defeat the negative effect of fear. Avoid procrastination as it would only lead to more doubt and fear. Make the positive step towards your goals and you will overcome fear. Recognise that your fear is nothing more than psychological. The panic, worry, tension and embarrassment you fear is as the result of your negative frame of consciousness. Fear can stop you from capitalising on opportunities. Do not allow fear to prevent you from achieving your goals in life. No one is born with super-confidence genes. Confidence is acquired and developed. Your action will cure it. Indecision and postponement will only add to your fear. When next you are faced with a difficult situation, don't bury your face in the mud. Ask your consciousness to guide you to what you need to do. Hope is a starting point. But hope needs action to win victories.

Next time you experience a small or large fear, control your consciousness and look for the answer to this soul searching question: 'What type of action can I take to overcome my fear?' Understand the cause of your fear, and take positive action. Postponement will enlarge your fears. Hesitation will increase your fear. It will only take ten seconds of courage to make that all important first positive step toward action to overcome your fear. Be decisive. Take immediate action now!

Within your consciousness lies the *Ultimate Power* to overcome any fear you may have. Change your attitude from negative to positive. Overcome the fear of losing by strong belief that you can win. Overcome the fear of failure with the *Ultimate Power* of success affirmation. Start now to see the positive side of any event in your life. Every event in your life carries with it an element of opportunity. Reactivate your consciousness to appreciate the positive in any situation. Always look on the bright side of life. Begin to see every event in your life as a springboard to

> *Today is the greatest day of your life. Make the best of it. Use your* Ultimate Power of Choice *to choose to live today as the greatest day of your life. Utilize your* Ultimate Power of Action *to change your life today, no matter how little. Do something, no matter how small, within the twenty-four hours of today that will bring you inner bliss, joy, happiness, and hope for a better tomorrow.*

success. Get rid of the guilt consciousness. Learn from every experience and prosper. Yesterday is history – learn from it or forget it entirely. Don't worry about tomorrow. Rather set your sights on high and wonderful goals towards tomorrow. Today is the greatest day of your life. Make the best of it. Use your *Ultimate Power* of choice to choose to live today as the greatest day of your life. Utilise your *Ultimate Power* of action to change your life today, no matter how little. Do something, no matter how small, within the twenty-four hours of today that will bring you inner bliss, joy, happiness, and hope for a better tomorrow. You are the sum total of your consciousness. You are the product of your imagination.

Resolve now to sow in your consciousness the seeds of courage, positiveness, hope, love for yourself, and strong belief in your ability to win, and you will conquer fear to *stretch your consciousness to succeed.*

> *Resolve now to sow in your consciousness the seeds of courage, positiveness, hope, love for yourself, and strong belief in your ability to win, and you will conquer fear.*

The Ultimate Formula

- You will have sufficient strength and wisdom for all your success needs if you encounter struggle and conquer it.

- Nothing worthwhile in life is ever achieved without a struggle. Life is a struggle and the rewards go to those who encounter difficulty, face it squarely, overcome it and move on to the next challenge. Every truly successful person you will find has been through a struggle in his or her life, and conquered. You too will conquer your struggle and succeed if you strongly believe.

- Embrace your struggle, do not avoid it, and you will learn, grow and succeed.

- Always be true to yourself. It doesn't matter what others may think about you. Conduct yourself with full regard to the ultimate invisible power which can guide you to wonderful glory, fame, and riches.

- You must show a keen interest in people, especially those with whom you have something in common and cultivate a bond of friendship with them.

- Your sincerity will be rewarded by self-satisfaction, respect and a spiritual ability to live with yourself twenty-four hours a day.

- Hope for a better tomorrow. Uplift the *Ultimate Power* of your consciousness with faith and believe that nothing is impossible.

- You must overcome fear to reach your goal. Control your fear. Do not allow fear to rule your decisions and actions.

- Take that courageous and bold first step toward your goal. Procrastination will only increase your doubt and fear. Take immediate action and kill your fear. Be willing to take risks when sound logic shows they are necessary.

Stretch Your Consciousness Now

Triumph Notes

PROGRESS • ACHIEVEMENT • SUCCESS

Challenge Notes

PLANS • TARGETS • HOPES

Chapter *4*

Change Your Environment Right Now

You are living in the prison created by your consciousness. Expand your consciousness now and break away from the rusty prison bars that hold you back. You possess the *Ultimate Power* to break away from abject poverty. You possess the same God-given *Ultimate Power* of intelligence and reason as the most successful person you know. But the difference is that the successful person is able to develop and tap into that *Ultimate*

> *Re-programme and re-activate your creative consciousness to succeed.*

Source on a regular basis. You too can do that. It's never too late to succeed in something.

You can harness the *Ultimate Power* of your consciousness by developing the positive you. As stated in the introduction, this book is not a story handbook. This book is not meant to mellow, or calm you down. The sole purpose of this book is to re-activate the *Ultimate Power* of your consciousness to achieve the greatest and most wonderful success you can ever imagine. Take this book to your heart, believe in the message, for every line in it contains pure, unadulterated truth, and facts of life. You will find in it the *Ultimate Power* to develop, re-programme and re-activate your creative consciousness to succeed.

Change your environment by changing your belief

system. Believe in greater things and wonderful things will begin to happen to you. I began to believe in greater things as a child. The *Ultimate Power* of my belief changed my environment from poverty stricken childhood in the war-torn famine-stricken Biafra and ghetto (slum) environment, to 'bright lights, big city', to academic excellence; to amateur competitive sports – Soccer, American Football, Body-Building; to finance and administrative career success – involving civil service, industry and commerce; entrepreneurial initiatives and vision. Anyone can change their environment. You too can change your environment no matter how low you may find yourself. No time is ever too late. Start right now to implant positive seeds into your consciousness. Believe big and your circumstances will alter dramatically to bigger things. Reading this book is a positive step in the right direction. Believe in the message for it is universal truth. You possess the *Ultimate Power to change your environment right now!*

> *Anyone can change their environment.*

Free your mind and the rest will follow

One of the ingredients of success is an open mind. You can alter your consciousness through an open mind. Open your consciousness to new ideas, concepts, and people. Unlock that door that imprisons your consciousness. An open mind is a free mind. You will achieve success through an open mind.

Ignorance is a disease in itself.

Be tolerant, and communicate with an open mind. Open up your consciousness and achieve the *Ultimate Power* of vision and positive perception. Ignorance is a disease in itself. Allow your consciousness, that unhindered freedom, to act for you. You will remain static if you don't cultivate a positive attitude and open mind. With an open mind, you will make progress, and will benefit from the opportunities progress offers. Whatever your consciousness can conceive and believe, you can achieve. With an open mind, you will achieve extraordinary success in your personal life, work, profession or business.

You will remain static if you don't cultivate the positive attitude of open mind.

There must be one thing you can do better than anyone else you know.

Open up your mind to possibilities. Stop doubting your abilities to achieve great things. You are as good as anyone you know, if not better. There must be one thing you can do better than anyone else you know. Focus on your desires, and belief. Keep your eye on the ball at all times and you will achieve your set goals.

Have faith in yourself, faith in your fellow human

beings, and faith in the Almighty Creator who has laid out the universal foundation for all of us. Get rid of prejudice and superstitious beliefs. Examine your personality. Open up your consciousness and come out into the light. Start to make decisions based on reason and logic rather than on emotion and prejudice. Cultivate the all important attitude of listening closely, attentively, and thoughtfully to what the other person says. Seek to get your facts right. Stop depending on hearsay and rumours for your decisions.

Stimulate and influence your consciousness with fresh thoughts. Your consciousness is imprisoned by the social and cultural environment you live in. You can break away from this by expanding your consciousness with positive ideas and desires. Sweep aside the bars of prejudice. Open your mind and be free to achieve financial and personal success. *Free your mind now and riches will follow!*

> *Seek and get your facts right. Stop depending on hearsay and rumours for your decisions.*

The Ultimate Power to get along

Your natural ability will blossom within the right company. Like does attract like. Whatever you sow, you shall reap. You get what you give. Your positive image will attract positive people around you. These are simple and well-known facts of life. Why waste your life within a negative environment, when you know that within your consciousness lies the *ultimate blessing* and ability to love and be loved, give and receive, smile and be smiled at, appreciate others and be appreciated.

Cultivate the positive virtues of integrity, sincerity, humility, courage, justice and modesty. Your ability to get along harmoniously with others will enable you to alter your environment and achieve incredible success.

You possess in your consciousness the *Ultimate Power* of friendship. Keep your friendship under constant renewal and turn your environment into a resourceful one. Make fresh acquaintances as you go through life to prosper. Do not speak unkind words about anyone. If you cannot say something positive about someone, do not say anything at all. You should always find something fresh to appreciate and admire about someone and tell the person so. Be grateful and compliment your friend.

> *Within your consciousness lies the ultimate blessing and ability to love and be loved, give and receive, smile and be smiled to, appreciate others, and be appreciated.*

Gain the affection of your friend by making sacrifices. Commit some of your time, thought and money to your friend. Offer someone you love the gift of friendship – give what is wanted of you, and no more. Think positive thoughts about your friends and loved ones. The *Ultimate Power* of your consciousness will guide you to what to do to make your friendship a resourceful one. Positive beliefs will bring you opportunities.

Get out more. Meet other people. Expand your consciousness. Mix more freely, and widen your interest. Get into the positive habit of doing something for others without expecting anything in return. The *Ultimate Power* of nature has its way and time of rewarding you. Give of yourself to others, and don't hold back. Believe in the *Ultimate Power* of your consciousness to lead you to friendships that can help you achieve extraordinary and wonderful success.

> *Your ability to get along harmoniously with others will enable you to alter your environment and achieve incredible success.*

The Ultimate Power of modelling yourself for success

Your consciousness will believe whatever you model it to believe. Believe you will be great, and you will be. Believe you are beautiful, and handsome, and you will begin to see the inner beauty in you. 'Beauty is in the eye of the beholder.' Believe in magic and you will begin to achieve magical things. Believe in miracles and you start to notice miraculous things.

You possess the *Ultimate Power* to be as good, even better, than the next person. You must believe in yourself first. There is no limit to what you can achieve through the *Ultimate Power* of right modelling. No worthwhile and true success is by accident. You must have values and beliefs. You must have the positive motivation and inspiration to achieve success. Every successful person was inspired and influenced by someone. What you are today is as a result of your belief system. Your belief system may have come from parental or family models, native environment, and traditional beliefs.

> *Every successful person was inspired and influenced by someone. What you are today is as a result of your belief system.*

You can change your current circumstances by remodelling your consciousness. Expand your consciousness beyond its current parameters. Examine the lives of the successful people you know. Tap into their resources. Model yourself around someone or some people you know who are highly successful. Make that person your hero, or

> *Model yourself around someone or some people you know who are highly successful.*

heroes if more than one person. Admire the achievements of the successful person, but do not worship him or her. Believe, strongly believe you can be as good, even better. Give yourself the opportunity to achieve greater success than your heroes.

Everybody must have a hero. However, having a hero is not enough. You must have a strong desire to achieve great and wonderful things like your hero. You must also aspire to become somebody else's hero, and there are many ways that you can be. You can, through cultivating and living a positive life, be a hero and inspiration to your children until they are mature enough to expand and add to their list of heroes. Through positive attitude, you can be the right inspiration and hero to your brother, sister, cousin, nephew, colleague at work and partner in business, employees (if you are an employer), and to your neighbour.

Part of the *Ultimate Power* of your consciousness is the power to emulate. Activate your God-given power to emulate the lives of successful people and you too can succeed. To achieve this, you must first determine your innermost talent. Once you know where your talent lies, and have strong belief in your inner ability, find people who have achieved success in that area and tap into their resources. Study the lives of the successful people you know. In no time, the *Ultimate Power* of your consciousness will activate your inner talent and ability. You will harness your innermost resources to achieve success beyond the belief of the ordinary mind.

> *Emulate the lives of successful people and you too can succeed.*

Choose your heroes carefully. Model yourself around the most positive personalities and great achievers. The world is full of incredible successes.

There may be about two per cent of incredibly successful people in the whole world, but the world's population is about five billion which makes the ratio about two hundred million wonderfully successful people. This book is not about mathematical facts. But the point is that there are plenty of wonderfully successful people on whom to model your talent and admiration.

Look up to the greats; admire them rather than worship them; emulate them; replicate their achievements – *model yourself right and excel.*

> *Model yourself around the most positive personalities and great achievers.*

The Ultimate Formula

- Live harmoniously with others, because your ability to get along harmoniously with others will greatly improve your chances of success.

- You must be loyal to those to whom loyalty is due. Do unto others as you would want others to do unto you. Love your neighbour as yourself.

- You will achieve the *Ultimate Power* to succeed with the all important virtues of integrity, sincerity, humility, courage, justice and modesty.

- Sacrifice some of your time, thought, and money to your friends. Offer someone you love the gift of friendship – give what is wanted of you, and no more.

- Change your environment by re-modelling your consciousness toward the positive.

- Model yourself around someone or some people you know, who has triumphed over adversities and achieved wonderful things.

- Admire the great success of others, but do not worship them. Give yourself the opportunity to achieve great things by sincerely believing that you can be as good, even better than your heroes.

- Open your mind. Broaden your consciousness to the wonderful opportunities around you.

- Have faith in yourself, faith in your fellow human beings and faith in the Almighty Creator.

- Do not allow the negative powers of superstition, doubt, prejudice, greed, hearsay, rumours and emotion to influence your decisions.

- Be colour blind. Don't be shallow.

- Expand and uplift your consciousness positively and *change your environment right now!*

Triumph Notes

PROGRESS • ACHIEVEMENT • SUCCESS

Challenge Notes

PLANS • TARGETS • HOPES

Chapter 5

Activate your Ultimate Power of Belief

Your belief is the golden key which you can use to open the door to wonderful opportunities and achievements. Your belief will guide you toward the means to achieve your set goals. Your beliefs will help you see what you want and energise you to get it.

> *Believe in success and you will receive the Ultimate Power to achieve great success.*

Belief is the ultimate directing force in your consciousness. Change your beliefs and change your behaviour. Start now to believe in success and you will receive the *Ultimate Power* to achieve great success. Believe in possibilities and you can accomplish anything.

Your belief will determine how much of your potential you will be able to tap. You will harness your potential with belief in your abilities. Begin to see yourself as nothing less than successful. Promise yourself that you will succeed.

Change the way you see yourself. Start believing more in yourself. Start now to love yourself more. Start now to appreciate the *Ultimate Power* of your consciousness to achieve anything. Stop rejecting yourself for not being perfect. Stop looking down on yourself for not conforming to society's current fashion or tradition. Get

> *Begin to see yourself as nothing less than successful.*

away from the group thing and start doing your own thing. Accept yourself for what you are. Recognise the fact that you are in a state of growth and you can always learn more and can perform better. Turn your imperfection to challenge and opportunity to achieve growth.

Start now to believe in yourself, and take charge of your life. Begin now to reshape your self-image by respecting yourself and liking yourself more. Don't dwell on your past failures, and start seeing yourself at your best. Cultivate an 'I can', 'I will', 'I am' a success awareness and up-lift the *Ultimate Power* of your consciousness to appreciate the wonderful opportunities around you.

> *You are in a state of growth, and you can always learn more, and can perform better.*

> *Take charge of your life.*

Cultivate the 'I will' attitude to activate the *Ultimate Power* of your consciousness to take action toward achievement of your set goal. Cultivate the incredible power of 'I am a success' and you will activate the *Ultimate Power* of belief to achieve extraordinary success.

> *Reshape your self-image by respecting yourself and liking yourself more.*

Wake up to the confident you

Resolve now to give yourself that inner confidence to succeed in any chosen field. Have confidence in yourself and your abilities to succeed. Know what you want, and be determined to get it. Refuse to accept the word impossible. Your consciousness possesses the *Ultimate Power* which you can tap and direct to your desired goal. Stop looking down on yourself. Determine never to sell yourself short.

Your consciousness will accept any message you give to it. Your consciousness will believe everything you tell it, and will act according to your command. You can therefore put the *Ultimate Power* of your consciousness to work in a positive and goal-orientated frame. Do not allow your consciousness to dwell upon poverty, failure, ill health, and all the things you do not want. You must condition your consciousness with positive and strong desires. Train your consciousness to serve you in

> *Begin to reason for yourself. Stop allowing outside influence to control your thought, emotion, and behaviour.*

everything you do, and you will achieve self-confidence.

Learn to be in control of your consciousness. Start trusting yourself more. Begin to reason for yourself. Stop allowing outside influences to control your thoughts, emotions, and behaviour. You will not achieve self-confidence by doing anything because 'A' or 'B' is doing it. Learn to trust your own instinct. Start paying your own way through everything. You must organise the *Ultimate Power* of your consciousness to be able to make up your mind about anything – that way you achieve self-confidence. Get away from group structure, and traditional beliefs. Be a team player and team leader, and not a team follower. Be in the team. Be a participant. Be active and not passive. Make your own mark. Don't wait for others to start the action before you can join. Support your team, but follow your conscience.

Your choice of peer group, or friends, will greatly determine the level of your success in life. Get away from any friendship which does not give you freedom to make your own decisions. A true friend will respect your spaces, and freedom of choice. A true friend will not control your decisions and activities. Feed your consciousness with what you want.

> *A true friend will not control your decisions and activities.*

Avoid moaners and gossipers. Moaners will always look at the problems and not the solutions. Moaners never accept responsibility. Moaners will always blame the mistakes of others for their misfortune. Moaners will always look for an alibi to avoid their responsibility. Moaners will always speak of the cost and value of their expenses, but will never mention the greater benefit they were expecting from the anticipated profit. The moaner focuses on the negatives. The moaner is only interested in profit, and will quit or blame everybody else at the slightest sign of a challenge.

Change your attitudes and begin to live more positively. Cut down on your intake of any stimulant, such as alcohol or cigarettes. It is advisable to avoid these substances entirely. But if you really have to drink alcohol or smoke tobacco, cut down your consumption to a minimum. Avoid non-medically recommended drugs. You do not need to stimulate your consciousness or physical body with any form of artificial substance or hard drug. You can easily stimulate the *Ultimate Power* of your creative con-sciousness with positive desires and resourceful attitude. Cultivate the habit of reading on a regular basis. Expand your reading material. Read more self-development books and materials. Read your business or professional journal. Read your favourite fiction novel. Cut down on your television time and you will find time to read more. Reading will activate the *Ultimate Power* of your consciousness to enable you to achieve self-confidence, and you will become a leader in your chosen field.

> *You do not need to stimulate your consciousness or physical body with any form of artificial substance or hard drug. You can easily stimulate the Ultimate Power of your creative consciousness with positive desires and resourceful attitude.*

Wake up to the triumphant you

You will attain success through the *Ultimate Power* of the positive you. Take control of your positive self, and become triumphant. Know that within your consciousness lies the *Ultimate Power* to overcome any unpleasant situation or habit. Harness the *Ultimate Power* of your consciousness to overcome any adversity and become triumphant again and again.

> *Your most profound happiness should lie not in content, but in continued struggle to succeed.*

You will overcome any handicap situation by concentrating on the situation you want and not the situation you are attempting to overcome. Master the *Ultimate Power* of your consciousness to achieve great and wonderful things and you will be triumphant. Recognise the fact that the greatest of successes is achieved through struggle. Your most profound happiness should lie not in content, but in continued struggle to succeed.

> *Put your **Ultimate Power** of positive self to work to create all the joy you desire, all the riches you need for peace and happiness, and all the will to keep your physical body free from ailments.*

Galvanise your *Ultimate Power* of positiveness to triumph over any adversity. Wake up to your positive self. Transform your failures, defeats and adversities into a wealth of experience and intelligence. Join the elite of extraordinarily successful people by a 'never say die' attitude when next you are faced with failure or defeat. Do not give up and quit. You can turn every adversity to potential opportunity.

Become better acquainted with that *Ultimate Power* of positive self which lies in your consciousness. Put your *Ultimate Power* of positive self to work to create all the joy you desire, all the riches you need for peace and happiness, and all the will to keep your physical body free from ail-ments. The greatest achievers of all time are those who achieved the seemingly impossible by tapping into the *Ultimate Power* of their positive self and directing it to definite ends in a spirit of perfect faith.

> *Turn every misfortune to valuable experience.*

Wake up to your challenges. Accept your responsibilities. Open up your eyes and see the opportunities that lie within any failure. Turn every misfortune to valuable experience. Tap into your positive self and you will be triumphant over any adversity.

Wake up! *Stand up for your rights! Stand up for your natural right to succeed!*

Your Ultimate Power to look ahead

Get into the habit of visualising a bigger and brighter future for yourself and your loved ones. Set your sights to the highest, and you will in turn utilise your goals to help you grow. Become optimistic about your goal and all your activities. Have hope for a better tomorrow. Remember, the important thing is not where you are now but where you want to get to.

> *The important thing is not where you are now but where you want to get to.*

Cultivate the essential habit of optimism. Your chances of success will be greatly enhanced by the *Ultimate Power* of optimism. Learn to look ahead positively. Your optimism and positive hope for a better tomorrow will help you develop the essential traits of enthusiasm, faith, decisiveness, a good sense of humour, contentment, flexibility and the ability to overcome fear.

Stop worrying about the bad things that might befall you, and spend more time each day relishing the desire for pleasant events that will come to you. You will get into the habit of optimism by thinking and believing in your wonderful and great desires.

> *Every successful person looks ahead with optimism.*

Every successful person looks ahead with optimism. Your positiveness and optimism will lead you to like-minded optimists. 'Like does attract like.' You will begin to relate with people who look towards tomorrow with hope. You will develop a healthy, peaceful and contented consciousness. Optimism is a success in itself. A lot of materially wealthy people can be failures physically, mentally and spiritually because of their constant pessimism towards life.

Look ahead fearlessly, honestly and with optimism and you will find victory in every defeat. Be bold and meet your future head-on. Analyse and weigh up the factors with a clear and open mind. Decide upon your course of action with your head high and chest upward; for you will find that the future holds nothing you ever need to be afraid of. You possess the *Ultimate Power to look ahead with great hope!*

The Ultimate Formula

● Believe big and you will achieve big and wonderful success.

● Stop looking down on yourself. Start loving yourself more. You are not perfect. Nobody is perfect. You are in a state of growth. You can always learn more, improve yourself and perform better.

● Restore your self-confidence. Trust your consciousness to guide your decisions. Be your own person – bold, brave and sincere with yourself.

● Avoid non-medically recommended drugs, and excessive consumption of alcohol and tobacco.

● Be optimistic and look ahead with faith, hope and great expectation.

Activate Your Ultimate Power of Belief

Triumph Notes
PROGRESS • ACHIEVEMENT • SUCCESS

Challenge Notes
PLANS • TARGETS • HOPES

Chapter 6

The Ultimate Power to Set Your Goals and Face New Challenges

You must galvanise your life with fresh and new challenges. Set yourself new targets and goals. You will find great energy with your sights set towards new targets. Your talents will diminish if you do not utilise and apply it to achieve fresh success. Renew your goals and start growing again. Use goals to help you grow.

> *You will be lost in life's shuffle if you do not plan and set yourself fresh goals.*

Establish fresh goals and you will not wander through life. If you stop setting new goals your consciousness will become dormant and die. Remember, the important thing is not where you are at this moment, but where you want to get. You will be lost in life's shuffle if you do not plan and set yourself fresh goals.

Set out your plan in writing. Get into the habit of writing out your plans for tomorrow, today! Cultivate the habit of committing your plans in writing – nature has its way of implanting your plans and commitment into your consciousness. The *Ultimate Power* of your consciousness will magnify your plan into the right actions for your success.

Plan ahead. Set out in writing your plans for the next three months, six months, twelve months, two years, five years, and ten years. There are many self-help books and materials on specialised, different techniques, guides and forms for setting out your goals.

Read as many self-help books as possible – you will find each one of them a great help. Every self-help book you read will uplift and expand your consciousness. Each self-development book contains the unique experience, talent, and resources of the writer. Even the different titles, and headings can greatly awaken and expand the *Ultimate Power* of your consciousness to '*set your goals and face new challenges!*'

The Ultimate Power to set that goal, right now

There is no accident about success. Nothing happens just by chance. Someone or something has to make something happen. To succeed in anything, you must have definite action which must take careful planning and persistent action. You must condition your consciousness to believe in great success and you will achieve wonderful things. You must know where you want to go and set out the plan for getting there. If you have absolute faith in your ability, you will achieve wonderful success.

> *Highlight your desires - those things which after you achieve them would, in your opinion, make you feel fulfilled.*

Start now to define, in definite terms, what you want, how much of it you want and when you want to have it in your humble possession. Highlight your desires – those things which after you achieve them would, in your opinion, make you feel fulfilled.

Make out a clear plan by which you intend to attain your set goals and clearly state what you intend to give in return. Set out a time limit within which you intend to acquire your set desires.

Commit to memory your plans and goals. Pray, contemplate, and strongly believe that you have already received your desires. Give thanks and gratitude to the Almighty Creator for having received that which you have asked for. Believe, strongly believe and you shall receive.

Your little academic education, or lack of money must not discourage you from choosing any goal you desire for your life. Your *Ultimate Power* of definite purpose will help you turn the seemingly impossible into possibilities. This *Ultimate Power* is within your consciousness. You do not need money or academic qualification to tap into it. All you need is your inner will and initiative to harness that *Ultimate Power*.

Fill your consciousness with great desires. Contemplate regularly about your wonderful desires. Remove from your consciousness that which you do not want. Harness the *Ultimate Power* of your creative consciousness to set high goals. Whatever your consciousness can conceive, with definite planning, and strong belief, you can achieve. Within your consciousness lies the *Ultimate Power to set that goal, right now!*

The Ultimate Power to destroy the habit of procrastination

Putting off until tomorrow what you can do today is a dangerous habit. Harness the *Ultimate Power* of your consciousness and take initiatives to cure your procrastinating habit. People who have achieved extraordinary success think and move promptly on their personal initiative.

Each time you put off doing something that you can do now, for later, you cheat yourself. Resolving to do something later, which you could do now, is a classic sign of self-delusion. You must start putting an end to procrastination, now!

Take immediate action now! Initiate action now on your dreams and desires. Make a start and eliminate the anxiety you may have about any project. Your decisiveness and boldness of action will awaken the *Ultimate Power* of your consciousness to excel. Stop waiting for the perfect time for there is no perfect time. Waiting for the perfect time will immobilise your ability to succeed. Seize the moment right now! 'A lazy person is never lucky', goes an old saying. Have courage, take that all important first step toward your set goal and you will have the *Ultimate Power* to succeed.

> *Initiate action now on your dream, and desire. Make a start and eliminate the anxiety you may have about any project.*

Start now to make your contribution in life. The greatest achievers of all time are those who were able to make their mark conscientiously. Don't wait until all the odds are in your favour before you make your contribution to life. Become accountable to life and don't wait for life to account to you.

You will surely make mistakes along the way. No

one is perfect. Put your foot forward. If you fail, try again. Accept your mistake as a lesson in progress. Most extraordinarily successful people achieved their greatest progress through trial and error – they dared to fail time after time.

> *Don't wait until all the odds are in your favour before you make your contribution to life.*

Begin now to see your mistakes and failures as springboards to life's opportunities. You must try to learn from the past, but don't live in the past. Cultivate a positive attitude towards every event in your life.

> *You must try to learn from the past, but don't live in the past.*

Utilise the *Ultimate Power* of definite action and overcome the negative effect of procrastination. You possess the *Ultimate Power to destroy the habit of procrastination now!*

Your Ultimate Power to give and receive

Give of yourself to others, and nature will reward you in ways that your consciousness could never imagine.

Helping others solve their problems will help you solve your own. Your genuine desire to be of service to others will bring you immeasurable success.

> *By maintaining a positive and resourceful state of consciousness, you will be able to channel your talents and abilities in many ways to help others.*

Remember that what you share will multiply. Resolve now to share your talent and you will discover that you possess greater talents. Give and you shall receive. Give of yourself without asking for anything in return, and you will be blest immensely.

I am not advocating that you liquidate your resources and give all to some charity or religious organisation. You must look after yourself and family first. You can only give what you have.

There are so many ways you can lend a helping hand. The *Ultimate Power* of your consciousness will lead you to ways you can share your talent and resources. By maintaining a positive and resourceful state of consciousness you will be able to channel your talents and abilities in many ways to help others.

What you don't possess you can't give. If you fill yourself with love, you will love others. Start every day by declaring yourself a channel to the Almighty Creator. Ask the Almighty to direct your every thought and deed. Your inner peace and happiness will radiate as positive energy which will act as a channel to improve the life of the people around you and any other person you come in contact with.

Resolve to do something each day to help someone. The universal law requires that you do some act of service to others on a regular basis. Your effort on behalf of someone less fortunate will not only help that person, but will also add something of great value to the *Ultimate Power* of your consciousness to succeed. Give of yourself, share your own talent, so you too can be blest. Apply your *Ultimate Power to give and receive now!*

The Ultimate Formula

- Plan ahead. Set out in writing your desires. Desire big. It doesn't matter how incredible, or crazy your desires may seem at first. Whatever your heart desires, you shall receive. Be like a child again. Desire, and believe anything without worrying about how to get it.

- Commit to memory your plans and goals. Pray, contemplate and strongly believe that you have already received your desires.

- Don't put-off until tomorrow what you could do today. Take action. Make a start toward your goal and overcome the negative effect of procrastination.

- Give and you shall receive. Resolve to do something each day to help someone else, no matter how small.

Cut Your Own Firewood

Triumph Notes

PROGRESS • ACHIEVEMENT • SUCCESS

Challenge Notes

PLANS • TARGETS • HOPES

Chapter 7

Don't Squander Your Natural Talent

Resolve now to claim your birthright. Harness the *Ultimate Power* of your creative consciousness, become positive in your outlook, believe in yourself and your ability to achieve great success. Become more enthusiastic, expect great things and anticipate wonderful things.

Start your day with positive thoughts. Resist the influence of negative thoughts. Resolve not to allow negative thought into your consciousness. Your state of consciousness will determine the extent of your success.

When you really believe that something can be done, the *Ultimate Power* of your consciousness will help you find the talent to do it. Your belief will release your natural talent to succeed. The *Ultimate Power* of your consciousness will develop your talent to excel, if you believe.

Where there is a will, there is a way. Within your consciousness lies the *Ultimate Power* to harness your natural talent to achieve great things. Develop your natural talent, or it will go to waste. You possess the natural talent to achieve your heart's desire. But you must harness and apply it to achieve your set goals.

> *Develop your natural talent, or it will go to waste.*

Do not allow traditional thinking to freeze the *Ultimate Power* of your consciousness. *Traditional thinking is a dangerous enemy to the Ultimate Power of your creative consciousness*. Open your mind to new and fresh ideas. Break from fixed routines. Welcome new concepts and become receptive to fresh beliefs. Search for new and better ways of doing things. Cultivate progressive attitudes.

Believe you can do more and better, and the power of your creative consciousness will utilise your natural talent to show you the way. Capacity is a state of mind. How much you can achieve depends on how far you can expand the *Ultimate Power* of your consciousness to succeed.

Expand your consciousness. Stimulate the *Ultimate Power* of your consciousness. Associate with people of different occupational and social interests. Mix with people who can help you to think of new ideas, new ways of doing things. Read more positive materials, contemplate more, pray on a regular basis and harness your natural talents. Don't allow your natural talent go to waste. Don't squander it. Find something you are good at and start now to apply your natural talent. Everybody is good at something. It's what you do with what you have that counts. *Utilise your natural talent now; don't squander it!*

The Ultimate Power of contemplation

You must learn to control your mind to harness the *Ultimate Power* of your creative consciousness. You have got to close your consciousness to outside influence through the powers of silence and contemplation.

Stillness, silence and contemplation are the essential attributes to bring out the *Ultimate Power* of your creative consciousness.

> *Stillness, silence and contemplation are the essential attributes to bring out the Ultimate Power of your creative consciousness.*

You must cultivate the all important attitude of silence and contemplation. Contemplate on a regular basis. Listen to your inner self. Contemplate and you will become attentive and aware of the *Ultimate Power* of your creative consciousness.

Get away from a noisy environment. Go into silence on a regular basis. Noise saps your energy to focus and contemplate. Set out a private time for your contemplation. Go into a private room of your own, close the doors and windows, lock them if necessary; or you may take a walk to a peaceful location, sit and quietly contemplate.

You must find a quiet time to be alone, for at least thirty minutes, each day. Learn to silence your thoughts from the outside world. Empty and free your mind. Shut your eyes and just listen to the sound of your consciousness emanating from your head. There is a unique sound in your head which you will begin to hear when in silent, quiet contemplation. Get used to listening to this powerful sound of your consciousness on a regular basis. Appreciate this sound, for it is the raw, potent power of your creative consciousness.

Pay attention to your consciousness. Ask your consciousness to guide you, in everything you do, and it will do so. You will never go wrong, if you are guided by your consciousness. Talk things over with your consciousness. Your burden will be lightened. Every incredibly successful person I know practises the art of quiet contemplation or meditation. Most successful people will regularly go into their private retreat, away from everyone. They will come out refreshed and full of new and abundant energy.

Contemplate, and you will be rightly directed. Contemplate, and become purified. Contemplate, and you will be inspired to the highest endeavours. Request your consciousness to grant you the wisdom and understanding you need to succeed. Examine and reflect on your past negative outlook. Resolve to become positive in your outlook towards life today and towards the future. See yourself as successful and prosperous as you contemplate. Use the *Ultimate Power* of contemplation to control your thought habit. Visualise your great and wonderful future, and focus on your goals, and you will achieve incredible success.

> *Examine and reflect on your past negative outlook. Resolve to become positive in your outlook towards life today, and towards the future.*

The Ultimate Power of love

'Love is a platform upon which all ranks meet', goes a popular saying. You can achieve unimaginable success with the *Ultimate Power* of your consciousness to love. Love, and seek love. Fuel your desires for success with the *Ultimate Power* of love. The number one wisdom, and secret of successful life, is love. Remember this always, and you will prosper immensely.

> *The number one wisdom, and secret of successful life, is love.*

Fill your consciousness with love, and let it overflow. Embrace the low and the high, the ugly and the beautiful, the sinful and the righteous – love all the same. See no difference between white, black, or coloured people. See no difference between plant, animal, and angel. Everybody and everything are all part of the same. Everything and everybody is part of the *ultimate whole*. Everything forms part of the invisible atom of the *Ultimate Creator*. To be successful, you must do away with old attitudes and beliefs. Throw away hate, prejudice, and stereotypical beliefs and you will succeed and enjoy your success without guilt or fear.

The world is full of lovely things. Love every minute of your day. Love everything you do. Make loving an essential part of your life. Love yourself. Love everything that happens to you.

Love your neighbour, your family, friends, relatives. Resolve to bring happiness and joy to every living being without exception. Identify yourself with all lives, and do not deliberately harm, hurt, or take away any life. Develop your *Ultimate Power to love – give love, and be loved*.

The Ultimate Power to make the right impression, magnify your personality and be enthusiastic

You can transform your consciousness to make the right impression. Develop and expand your consciousness to become enthusiastic. Enthusiasm is a potent energy by which you transmit your personality to others. Remember, no one is born with a quality of enthusiasm. Enthusiasm is acquired through positive attitudes and beliefs. You too can nurture your consciousness to achieve an enthusiastic personality.

> *No one is born with a quality of enthusiasm. Enthusiasm is acquired through positive attitudes, and beliefs.*

The leaders, builders, doers and pioneers who help uplift our consciousness in many wonderful ways, and advance our civilisation, are people who are able to harness the *Ultimate Power* of enthusiasm and apply and magnify their personality positively. Put your personal magnetism to work for you in order to achieve great things. Make your own personal magnetism work for you, and you will achieve great success. Put the *power* of enthusiasm, and personal magnetism to work. Learn to exude and magnify self-confidence, spiritual strength, wisdom, and authority. Cultivate the positive attitude of meeting the gaze of others more directly, to clasp their hands warmly and firmly, to speak forthrightly and in a pleasant tone to capture the listener's interest.

You will develop self-esteem, positive self-image, and a feeling of being worthy through self-appreciation. Never look down on yourself. Have respect for yourself, and give yourself the sense of dignity. Respect others, their feelings, and space. Forgive yourself for your trespasses. Forgive others for their ignorance, mistakes and wrong doings. Get rid of the guilt consciousness. Stop feeling sorry for yourself. Wake up and say to yourself: 'I am a good person'; 'I am a success'; 'I am positive'; 'I am a winner'; 'I am lovely'; 'I am a wonderful person'; 'I possess a wonderful personality'. Go to your mirror and watch yourself do this. Get a tape-recorder and record your own voice, if possible. It doesn't matter where you do this exercise, or which means is available to you – the all important thing is to hear your own voice, and physically see yourself in

> *Never look down on yourself. Have respect for yourself, and give yourself the sense of dignity. Respect others, their feelings, and space. Forgive yourself for your trespasses. Forgive others for their ignorance, mistakes and wrong doings. Get rid of the guilt consciousness. Stop feeling sorry for yourself.*

the mirror while doing this important exercise. You will achieve the *Ultimate Power to be enthusiastic, magnify your personality, make the right impression and achieve wonderful success.*

The Ultimate Formula

- Within your consciousness lies the *Ultimate Power* to harness your natural talent. Tap into this ultimate source of energy and achieve wonderful things in your life.

- Do not allow traditional thinking to freeze the *Ultimate Power* of your creative consciousness. Open your consciousness to fresh and new ideas.

- Contemplate and prosper. Go into silence, listen to your consciousness and become attentive and aware of the *Ultimate Power* of your consciousness.

- Let your love overflow. Love yourself; love all lives; and love all things. See no difference between white, black, or coloured people; see no difference between plants, animals, and angels.

- Love every minute of your day. Love everything you do.

- Appreciate your self-worth, for you may be worth more than you know.

- Never, ever look down on yourself.

Triumph Notes
PROGRESS • ACHIEVEMENT • SUCCESS

Don't Squander Your Natural Talent

Challenge Notes

PLANS • TARGETS • HOPES

Chapter *8*

Break It Down

Discover what it is you truly want for your life. Your *Ultimate Power* of creative consciousness will pull you toward a meaningful purpose for your life. Focus on your desires and the *Ultimate Power* of your creative consciousness will help you rise above your fears and limitations.

Set your own standards. Do not be misled, or confuse yourself with another person's way of life. Use the successes of others to inspire yourself. Do not worship anyone. Respect and appreciate the achievement of others, but don't be

> *Trust your own consciousness for what is right for you.*

overwhelmed, or subdued by them. You must trust your own con-sciousness for what is right for you. You alone must decide what is worthwhile, and the value of your suc-cess. Use other people's success as an inspiration and role model.

Make the all important connection with the power of your consciousness and define your *ultimate mission.* Establish personal goals in all areas of your life. Confront your life head on. Accept

> *Decide what is worthwhile, and the value of your success.*

responsibility for your life. Utilise your skill and ability to make your mark in this life. Use your skills to solve your problems swiftly.

Become active in the game of life and stop being a negative spectator on the side-line. Commit yourself, participate in the game and you will score and win. Be courageous, bold and don't be afraid to take risks.

The Ultimate Power of dynamic and active patience

You must not let what you haven't got now deter you from what you believe you can achieve. Don't be blind to your true potential, and the opportunities around you. Learn to look at things not as they are, but as they can be. Don't be stuck with the present – visualise the big things that you want to achieve.

> *It is not what you have, but what you plan to get that counts.*

Expand the *Ultimate Power* of your creative consciousness to visualise and believe what can be, not just what is. Visualise big. It is not what you have, but what you plan to get that counts. Add value to yourself. Add value to other people.

Cultivate a dynamic belief system. Eliminate petty thinking. Don't concern yourself with trivial matters. Keep your eye on the big ball and score big goals. Think big and eliminate minor quarrels. Keep your focus on your goals. Focus big and you will no longer concern yourself with trivial and unimportant things. When you are faced with any negative thought, ask yourself: 'does it really matter?' The positive power of this attitude will help you avoid unnecessary quarrels at home, in traffic, in the supermarket, or at work. The mere fact that you have big goals, and a positive focus, will help you see things in a

> *Keep your eye on the big ball, and score big goals. Think big, and eliminate minor quarrels. Keep your focus on your goals. Focus big, and you will no longer concern yourself with trivial and unimportant things.*

different frame. You will start to view every situation

from a higher level. The minor things that used to annoy and upset you will no longer matter.

Your positive focus on the bigger things, with your dynamic and active patience to get to your goal, will help you overcome negative trivialities, such as jealousy, anger, greed, hate, and unnecessary attachment. Do not waste your energy on these negative habits. Nothing saps your natural energy and talent like them. Avoid them. Focus on your main desires. Focus on what counts as your goal, and you will prosper.

Be dedicated to your set goal. Be patient. Have the courage to change the things you can. Be willing to accept the things you cannot; and have the wisdom to know the difference. The more strongly and inspired you are about your desires in life, the more patience you will have to overcome obstacles. If you know where you are going in life, the *Ultimate Power* of nature will allow you to tolerate the little annoyances that will come between you and your goal. Concentration on your goal will provide the patience you need to achieve it. *He that can have patience and determination with a burning desire will prosper.*

> *The more strongly and inspired you are about your desires in life, the more patience you will have to overcome obstacles.*

The Ultimate Power to adapt yourself

You must learn to make the best use of every experience, whether pleasant or unpleasant. Be flexible. Develop the wisdom to know when you are wrong. You have the *ultimate right* to change your decision. Be humble. You can adapt to any condition through the virtues of humility, flexibility and courage to admit you are wrong.

> *Make the best use of every experience, whether pleasant or unpleasant.*

Be grateful for the blessings around you. You do not need to bend backwards and subject yourself to the whims and wills of others in order to be humble and flexible. Though you need to win the co-operation and friendship of others to be truly successful, do not worship others to prove your humility. Respect your fellow human beings, but don't worship anybody.

Develop the ability to take prompt action in seizing opportunities or solving problems. Have the wisdom to survey, research and assess a given situation swiftly and react to it on the basis of logic and reason with minimum emotion.

Cultivate the *ultimate force* of humility to find strength in times of failure. The attitude of humility will give you the wisdom to bear the loss of a loved one. Apply the *ultimate force of humility* to help create a better world. Within humility you will discover the seed of equivalent benefit in time of adversity and defeat.

Humility and flexibility enable one to face their struggles with courage, boldness, flexibility, and dignity. Try to be humble and grateful to those from whom you receive co-operation and assistance. Similarly, do your best to hold your head high, keep your chin up, and smile in difficult times.

You too possess the *Ultimate Power to adapt yourself to any event in your life, and move on!*

Count your blessings

You must learn to count your blessings and assets more often than you do your troubles and problems and put them uppermost in your consciousness. You should realise that many of your blessings are hidden treasures – they may seem like commonplace everyday items, qualities, or events that can easily be taken for granted. The simple example of this can be your health, or the love, admiration and faith your family has for you.

> *Many of your blessings are hidden treasures – they may seem like commonplace everyday items, qualities, or events that can easily be taken for granted.*

Continue to give thanks and praise to the *Ultimate* and *Almighty Creator* for nature's blessings. To do this, you must strive to conscientiously open your consciousness to see, know and appreciate your opportunities and the blessings of nature around you.

You must open up your consciousness, and become aware of the wonderful opportunities and blessings in your daily life. Give thanks and praise to the Almighty Creator. Let the first word that comes out of your mouth each morning be 'thanks and praise to the Almighty Creator', no matter what your condition. *Count your blessings now; give thanks and praise; for whoever shows gratitude, more shall be given.*

> *Become aware of the wonderful opportunities and blessings in your daily life.*

Do not use your current lowly condition as an excuse for hating yourself or anyone else. Do not use your current circumstances as an alibi for indulging in consumption of any harmful substance.

Resolve now to regard your problems as stepping stones to success – each one you overcome brings you closer to your goal. Recognise the fact that every bad situation could be worse. You must not curse your luck because you have no shoes, for there are many without even the feet to wear shoes.

> *Every bad situation could be worse. You must not curse your luck because you have no shoes, for there are many without even the feet to wear shoes.*

Learn to see every inconvenience as an adventure. Your problem, or bad experience is not unique or new. A lot of incredibly successful people have been there and excelled. *You are not alone.* Don't be shy to seek the advice and guidance of those who have acquired their knowledge and wisdom through struggle and true life experience.

The Ultimate Formula

- Discover what your true goals are. Do not confuse your goals with other people's success.

- Focus on the bigger things. Apply the principles of dynamic and active patience, rather than passive and inactive attitude.

- Be humble, flexible, and adapt yourself to any condition in which you may find yourself.

- Regard your problems as stepping stones to success.

- Count your blessings – give thanks and praise to the Almighty Creator.

Break it Down

Triumph Notes
PROGRESS • ACHIEVEMENT • SUCCESS

Challenge Notes
PLANS • TARGETS • HOPES

Chapter 9

Let's Do It

Develop the *Ultimate Power* of your creative consciousness to succeed. Build a consciousness of success now! Apply the universal principles in this book to help you uplift your consciousness to succeed in anything you truly desire. Every word in this book will uplift and ignite the *Ultimate Power* of your creative consciousness to excel. Believe it's message, for it is universal truth. Strongly believe that you possess the *Ultimate Power* to achieve your soul's desires. Make a definite promise to yourself that you will succeed, and so it shall be.

Start to see yourself as nothing but a success. The *Ultimate Power* of success consciousness will lead you to achieve great and wonderful things. You will achieve anything your heart desires with the *Ultimate Power* of success consciousness.

Remember that it is within your power to change your condition. You possess the knowledge and talent to succeed. Your knowledge and talent will be of no use until you make use of it.

> *Take advantage of the law of abundance. How much you will draw from the source of abundance depends entirely upon the level and height of success consciousness you develop.*

Raise your sights high. The amount of worldly goods you acquire will be in direct proportion to the heights to which you raised your sights. There is plenty of room at the top. The percentage of the population who are highly successful is about two per cent. With strong will and determination, you too shall reach the top.

Expand the *Ultimate Power* of your consciousness, and start to take advantage of the law of abundance. How much you will draw from the source of abundance depends entirely upon the level and height of success consciousness you develop. Do not allow doubt to discourage you. Hold on to the truth, and believe that riches will be yours and you will acquire riches beyond your imagination.

Clear your consciousness from 'sin' or 'guilt' beliefs. Get rid of the traditional ideas of sin. Such obsolete beliefs hold you back from moving forward. They make you feel you are not worthy of success. Accept your responsibility. Be humble to understand your mistakes and accept your wrongs – make corrections, if you can, and move forward. The element of 'sin – confess – or perish' is a dangerous control factor and hindrance to progress. Free your consciousness from 'sin', 'guilt', and 'doubt' factors and make a new start in your life. Open your consciousness to the windows of opportunities: *let's do it, now!*

The Ultimate Power to condition your consciousness

You can condition your consciousness to balance your life and your relationship with people and circumstances to attract whatever you desire. Your greatest potential lies in your capacity to believe. You can draw upon it to form the all important habit of maintaining a positive attitude.

Whatever your consciousness can conceive and believe, you can achieve. Harness and apply the *Ultimate Power* of your consciousness to believe and join the leaders and forerunners of civilisation, the builders of industry, the creators of empires, the revealers of the abundant energy made available to us by the Almighty Creator. You possess the *Ultimate Power* and privilege to condition and control your consciousness with any sort of desire and belief system.

> *Do not hoard your talent and resources. Employ what you have, or it will go to waste.*

Do not hoard your talent and resources. Employ what you have, or it will go to waste. Nothing stays the same. Everything changes – it's the natural way of the universe. Even our physical body changes with astonishing rapidity.

Focus your consciousness positively. Maintain a positive attitude and shape the course of your own destiny rather than drifting along at the mercy of adversity. Your consciousness is blest with the *Ultimate Power* to think, aspire and hope and to direct your life toward any goal. You must seize the opportunity to excel. Apply your talents and resources to good use, or you will lose them.

Set out your definite goals in life. Decide on the course you wish to take to attain your set goal. Take positive steps, one at a time, and you will discover that each positive step makes the next one easier. Do not stand still – choose to move upward towards success. *You possess the Ultimate Power to condition your consciousness to achieve great and wonderful things: take decisive action now – do it !*

The Ultimate Power to direct your consciousness

You possess the *Ultimate Power* to direct your consciousness to those things which matter most to you. Through the knowledge and tools you have acquired from reading this book, you now possess the *Ultimate Power of positive consciousness.*

Direct your positive consciousness to see a problem as an opportunity and a difficulty as a challenge. Your

> *See a problem as an opportunity, and a difficulty as a challenge.*

future will be determined by your positive consciousness of today. You must now place your feet firmly on the ground of the present moment. You will develop a productive, loving life by developing productive, loving moments. Your positive attitude, more than anything else, will determine your productive, loving moments.

During a business trip to Africa, the *Ultimate Power* of my consciousness was uplifted and expanded by an anonymous poem which I saw framed in a business centre I visited.

Take time to work –
it is the price of success.

Take time to think –
it is the source of power.

Take time to play –
it is the secret of perpetual youth.

Take time to read –
it is the fountain of wisdom.

Take time to be friendly –
it is the road to happiness.

Take time to love and be loved –
it is nourishment for the soul.

Take time to share –
it is too short a life to be selfish.

Take time to laugh –
it is the music of the heart.

Take time to dream –
it is hitching your wagon to a star.

Direct your consciousness towards the positive and you will create opportunities and overcome limitations. The most wonderfully successful people of all time are those who had the courage to take positive action. They are those who live their lives today, with the greatest of positiveness and enthusiasm, as if there is no tomorrow. The successful people are those who take charge of their lives by directing the *power* of their consciousness toward positive objectives and goals.

Don't allow cynics to force you into negative rationalisation and frantic resistance. The cynics are those who see more of the negative side of their own life. The cynic will envy any sign of progress in your life. The cynic will criticise your courage and effort towards the positive. The cynic will give you many negative reasons why you should not believe in the content of this book, or any other self-development material. The cynic could be your parents, spouse, relative, or a friend who has resigned themselves to a static frame of consciousness and sees no reason for desiring anything better. The cynic will provide you with alibis and reasons for not believing in yourself and the truths in this book.

It is a universally known truth that success is achieved through strong belief in oneself, and belief in the *Ultimate Power* of nature. You do not need a special academic certificate to succeed. Academic qualification may assist you in getting a job but it will not be the major factor that will make you *succeed* in that job. Only by positive attitude and strong belief in yourself will you truly succeed in anything. Many successful people were not gifted academically, or even had the opportunity to pursue full-time education. The greatest successes have been achieved by people who were able to pick themselves up at any level or condition, acquired knowledge and experience as they went along, and triumphed over adversities.

Utilise the *Ultimate Power* of your consciousness to believe in yourself, and your ability to achieve anything you strongly desire. Direct your consciousness towards a positive attitude, and you will succeed. *Direct the Ultimate Power of your consciousness positively to achieve great and wonderful success.*

> *Only by positive attitude and strong belief in yourself will you truly succeed in anything.*

The Ultimate Formula

● You have within you the *Ultimate Power* to direct your consciousness positively to perform any service you desire.

● Positive attitude will not only lead to ways to overcome obstacles, but will actually provide you with the tools to turn them into opportunities.

● The positive power of your consciousness will lead you to associate with people who are themselves positively conscious, and who will inspire and encourage you to reason and act positively.

● Your positiveness will attract to you opportunities for success.

Let's Do It

Triumph Notes
PROGRESS • ACHIEVEMENT • SUCCESS

Challenge Notes

PLANS • TARGETS • HOPES

Chapter 10

You are Not Alone – Don't Worry, be Happy

Learn to share your success and happiness with others. Use your wealth to enrich the lives of others as well as your own life and you will find true happiness. Share your blessings with others and be blest the more.

Your money can bring you happiness and peace of mind, but can also bring misery, anxiety and fear which makes it impossible to maintain peace of mind. Turn your money into a blessing and not a curse, by the way you use it.

> *Turn your money into a blessing, and not a curse, by the way you use it.*

'No man is an island to himself.' You are not alone. It's one thing to become rich, but to become rich in all of the great riches of life which make true happiness, is another thing. You are not rich in higher consciousness unless you acquire the way to permanent peace of mind.

> *You must fuel your ambition and desires with a selfless and sincere wish to be useful to others.*

Your desire for great and wonderful things is a positive and healthy thing. But you must fuel your ambition and desires with a selfless and sincere wish to be useful to others. Never seek riches and power for personal aggrandizement. Selfishness and greed lead to loneliness, and unhappiness.

Apply your talent and utilise your resources positively for the good of others. Start to see yourself as the temporary custodian of your life and riches. Become a positive channel for the blessings bestowed on you by the Almighty Creator. What you share will multiply. What you hoard will diminish, fade and die.

Each day resolve to share a hug, a kiss, or a smile with your loved ones and others you come into contact with. Share a good, positive story, or joke to make someone laugh. Share your talent for music and singing and put joy into a soul. Share your knowledge and experience and the power of your consciousness will expand the more.

All the incredibly successful people of our time are those who are unselfish with their talent, experience and resources. Recognise now that *you are not alone. Don't worry, be happy to share your talent and resources and you will be blest the more!*

> **Become a positive channel for the blessings bestowed on you by the Almighty Creator.**

The Ultimate Power to overcome defeat, and achieve peace of mind

Learn not to get angry with yourself when you lose or fail to succeed in something. Accept your difficulty as a challenge. See every defeat as a motivation to face your challenges. Turn your defeat and failure into potential opportunity. Try not to waste your energy being discouraged. When things don't go the way you planned, don't despair and don't waste your time berating yourself. Be humble in defeat, courageous, and flexible to a change of course. Make plans to win next time.

> *Focus on that which is pleasant.*

Ask yourself: 'what can I learn from this situation'; 'what can I do to change or improve this situation?; and 'what can I do to create better opportunities?'

Don't worry. Be happy. Have faith in the *Ultimate Power* of your consciousness. Give yourself peace of mind. The *Ultimate Power* of your consciousness will find answers to your needs.

> *There is no such reality as a permanent loss. For everything taken away, some thing of equal or greater importance and value replaces it – it could be something completely different from the thing we lost.*

Eliminate defeatist attitudes. Refuse to allow unpleasant thoughts into your consciousness. Focus on that which is pleasant. Train your consciousness to see the potential opportunity in every experience. Your experiences in life – good or bad – are not important in and of themselves. It is your reaction to those experiences which count.

It is a fact of life that before we find ourselves, we must undergo a series of disappointments, reverses, defeats and failures. You must discover that there is no such reality as a permanent loss. For everything taken away, something of equal or greater importance and value replaces it – it could be something completely different from what we lost. Most failures or defeats can be blessings in disguise that will force you to take positive action in life. This can lead you to greater opportunities, happiness, and peace of mind.

The Ultimate Power to have, hold and enjoy

Be rich, content, and happy in your consciousness. Learn to be content with whatever you have got at the moment. Have strong desire for wonderful things, but start by being happy with what you have got at this moment.

The powerful tools you have acquired from this book will help you become rich beyond your wildest dreams. Let your desires for riches be a value that endures – a thing you cannot lose – something that provides you with contentment, sound health, peace of mind and harmony within your soul.

Cultivate the all important health consciousness. 'A healthy body is a healthy mind', goes a wise saying. Eat and drink only the essential, healthy food and drink. Be moderate with your consumption habits. Avoid gluttony.

Take up any physical exercise that suits you – consult your doctor for advice, if possible. Get into the positive habit of regular physical exercise. There are numerous forms of exercise habits to choose from – stretching, walking, jogging, dancing, swimming, weight-training, and many more. You may choose to exercise privately in your own home, or join a group or club. Whichever is your preference, take positive action to start immediately and you will achieve the *Ultimate Power to have, hold, and enjoy your riches.*

> *Let your desires for riches be of values that endure – things you cannot lose – things that provide you with contentment, sound health, peace of mind and harmony within your soul.*

You will find greater joy, and happiness by helping

others to succeed. Avoid the negative attitudes of hate and envy. Do your best to love, and respect all mankind, and you will achieve the *Ultimate Power to have, hold, and enjoy your wealth.*

In your daily contemplation, or prayer, ask not for more riches, but for more wisdom with which to recognise, embrace and enjoy the great abundance of riches you already possess. Be free from greed, and share your blessings.

Do not slander anyone for any cause. Speak only honourable things about your fellow human beings and you will remain on good terms with your consciousness to guide you accurately to great and wonderful success.

The Ultimate Formula

- You must discipline your consciousness for success, for by constancy of purpose you will achieve wonderful things.

- Don't quit whenever the going gets tough, for one more step might lead you to triumphant victory.

- Put your thought habits to positive order and they will lead you to opportunities.

- Activate the *Ultimate Power* of your will and regain control of your life. Harness the *Ultimate Power* of your creative consciousness and use it to serve your needs.

- You will achieve freedom of body and mind, independence and financial security as the result of your personal initiative expressed through self-discipline.

- What you are now is as a result of your habits and state of consciousness.

- You can achieve anything as long as you don't give up on yourself.

Triumph Notes
PROGRESS • ACHIEVEMENT • SUCCESS

You are not Alone

Challenge Notes
PLANS • TARGETS • HOPES

Chapter 11

It's Your Life. Visualise it – What You Get is What You See

Whatever you are right now is a reflection of the mental image you have been holding of yourself. Utilise the *Ultimate Power* of visualisation to harness the powers of your creative consciousness to achieve anything you set your heart upon. If you are positive in your visualisation the things you desire will come to you.

Transform your life with the *Ultimate Power* of your consciousness to visualise whatever you desire. You must first know exactly what you want and when you want to have it. Remember also that the true value of success is whatever brings you peace and happiness. So be careful of what you visualise, for what you get is what you see. Let it be what will bring more value to your life.

> *The true value of success is whatever brings you peace and happiness.*

Do not limit your desires because you cannot see where the wonderful things are going to come from. Your feeling alone counts. Your feeling is *raw power*. Believe that you have already obtained your desire. Leave it to the *Ultimate Power* of your creative consciousness, with strong belief, and you will be led to endless ways to achieve success.

Commit your vision into a written form. Examine your notebook every day, and believe. Become obsessed with your desires. Visualise what you want so intensely, so fiercely, that you feel you cannot live without it. Any desire which is backed by strong emotion is potent, and *Ultimate Power*.

> *Any desire which is backed by strong emotion is potent, and Ultimate Power.*

Visualise with strong emotion and believe, and you will achieve success beyond your expectation. Be like a child – ask for anything in this world. Don't worry or care about where or how it's going to come about.

Learn to make good use of your private room. Get into the all important habit of visualising the things you desire. Be particular and specific with your desires. Name them, and repeat over and over again the name of the things you want. Visualise them first thing in the morning, at work in your locked room, at night before retiring, and as you lie in bed. Dismiss any thoughts of obstacles. Don't contemplate failure. See yourself as having received all you asked for. Great and wonderful things will start to happen to you. They may appear, at first, as coincidences but they are simply the working out of the pattern which you started with the weavings of the *Ultimate Power* of your creative consciousness.

Cultivate a rich attitude. Learn to live your life today as the richest day of your life. Be enthusiastic. Be happy and show a feeling of expectancy. Be humble, and grateful for what you already have. Be courageous, bless your day and bless your present condition. Do not be resentful of anything and show patience and tolerance in your approach towards life. Start loving and giving. Stop hating, losing your temper and being selfish, and great and wonderful things will start to happen to you – your consciousness will become receptive to miraculous opportunities.

Resolve now to make contemplation, or meditation an important part of your daily existence. Visualise.

Communication with your consciousness is more than a two-way conversation. *It's your life. Visualise it – what you get is what you see!*

> **Bless your day and bless your present condition.**

The grateful, and gracious you

You must be grateful for all that you receive. Be grateful for the big things, the little things and just for being alive each moment. Your gratitude will open up the *Ultimate Power* of your consciousness to a dignified, gracious and joyous experience.

Arrogance and ignorance are dangerous and negative attitudes to possess. Never allow arrogance and ignorance to prevent you from giving thanks and praise both for the human and divine help you receive. Gratitude will enhance your personality with magnetic charm and you will gain the *Ultimate Power* to open your consciousness to infinite intelligence. Positive attitudes of gratitude and graciousness will help you develop a courtly and dignified personality.

Become gracious and dignified. Be creative and surprise your loved one, friend, boss, client, or creditor by writing a simple note telling them how grateful you are for the opportunities their love, friendship, understanding, care, and affection, offers you.

Don't neglect those who are closest to you – your spouse, relatives, and those you associate with daily – you might be more indebted to them than you realise.

Verbalise your gratitude to your family on a regular basis, and you will rejuvenate the *Ultimate Power* of positive love in the household.

> *Find new and unique ways to express your gratitude, not necessarily by gift.*

Give thanks and praise to the Almighty on a daily basis for the blessings in your life. Examine and compare circumstances and events in your life against what they might have been – you will become aware that no matter how bad things might seem, they could be much worse; and you should be grateful that they are not.

On a regular and daily basis, use 'thank you'; 'I am

grateful'; and 'I appreciate' to add courtesy to your expressions. You will always find something to be grateful for. Become more thoughtful. You will find new and unique ways to express your gratitude, not necessarily by giving a gift. Finding some time from your precious busy life to spend in showing your gratitude will be worthwhile. By expressing a simple gratitude, you make a big investment in your future.

There is no such thing as an overall self-made billionaire or millionaire. Everyone receives help along the road to success, no matter how little. Though the journey of success involves personal initiative, enthusiasm, and individual strength in struggle, a little help here and there is always involved. But whatever you do, never live for the past. Get rid of the traditional mentality that binds you to worship somebody due to their past favours to you. Do not carry with you a guilt consciousness of past favours: for all the good intent, express your gratitude whenever you can, but do not subject your consciousness to the feeling of guilt and an inferiority complex to someone because he or she may have helped you in the past. Remember, for every good thing a person does to someone else, nature has many ways of according equivalent reward. Express your gratitude however you can; but don't live forever as if you owe your whole life to someone because of what they had done for you in the past. If someone does you a favour with sincerity of purpose, without ulterior motive or a hidden agenda for their own benefit, that person is sure to receive nature's reward in greater benefit.

On a daily basis, resolve to renew the *grateful, and gracious you* for there is always a reason to be grateful.

> *For every good thing a person does to someone else, nature has many ways of according equivalent reward.*

The Ultimate Formula

● Visualise, contemplate, or meditate to transform the *Ultimate Power* of your creative consciousness to achieve wonderful success in your life.

● Don't limit the *Ultimate Power* of your consciousness to desire the greatest things because you cannot, at first, see where they will come from.

● Learn to daily give thanks and praise for both the human and divine help you receive. Be courtly, dignified and gracious.

● You will reap what you sow. Learn to do unto others as you wish them to do unto you. Think of others as you wish them to think of you.

Triumph Notes

PROGRESS • ACHIEVEMENT • SUCCESS

It's Your Life

Challenge Notes
PLANS • TARGETS • HOPES

Chapter **12**

The Only Way is Up

The universal principles in this book give you the tools and the *Ultimate Power* to become as rich as your heart desires. The powerful message in this book has worked time and time again; it is working, and will continue to work.

Through the *Ultimate Power* of this book, you have now in your possession a signed blank cheque which you may fill out for any amount you wish – any amount your beliefs can perceive.

Let us consider a simple situation whereby a legitimate cheque for £500,000 arrives in the post for you. Normally, this cheque will take between five to ten days for the bank to clear. In the meantime, you will feel that you have this money. Your actions from the moment you saw that cheque, your attitude and behaviour will reflect the fact that you own £500,000. You will begin to reason and act with optimism. You may not have any money in your pocket at the moment, with many debts to pay, but you will start acting rich and living your life with hope and enthusiasm, regardless.

> *By gaining the richness consciousness you are rich no matter how many or how few worldly goods you may possess*

What this book has given you is the *Ultimate Power* to activate and expand your consciousness to believe in yourself and your ability to acquire the riches you may desire. So, by gaining the richness consciousness you are rich no matter how many or how few worldly goods you may possess at this moment – you now know that it is within your power to manifest any riches according to the height of your belief.

You do not have to go about boasting or pretending to be rich. Be humble and dignified with your success consciousness. Your family, relatives, and friends will notice the progress you are making; they will know that you are rich by your changed attitude, enthusiasm and belief system.

Get into money consciousness. Make yourself a channel, a magnet, by keeping your consciousness open and alert. Speak to your consciousness every day and ask for money – wealth – ask incessantly and believe so much that it is coming that you can hardly contain your state of bliss.

> *Make yourself a channel, a magnet by keeping your consciousness open and alert.*

Develop a billionaire consciousness. Get excited about it as though you have been informed that billions of pounds are coming to you. Keep on asking, and you will get it. Don't worry if it doesn't come at the time you wanted it or in the form you wanted it; pass it as a test, learn and continue to believe, and don't accept defeat. You will get what you ask for with positive belief.

Get into the habit of loving money. It is not wicked to love money, as traditional thinking may like you to believe. But you must not, because of money, hold anyone to bondage. If you want to have money and behold, never loan money to anyone

> *What you do to anyone, you will get back.*

– give it. Get into the richness consciousness. To lend money to someone and exact interest is to put that person in bondage. Don't worry if the money you gave is not returned to you. You will receive money in other ways by letting that person have the money which he or she may owe you.

Do not resort to harassment, force or character assassination because someone owes you money. You will be putting yourself under the law when you resort to pressure and threatening measures against someone who owes you money. You will only create fear and block their path to success. What you do to anyone, you will get back. You will find yourself indebted to someone else in a strange circumstance – the law of nature forces back to us what we give. If you want to be truly rich and enjoy your richness, never hold anyone to ransom for the sake of money.

Cultivate the habit of saying to yourself, at daily and regular intervals: 'I am rich'; 'I am rich'; 'I am rich'. The *Ultimate Power* of your creative consciousness will recognise this powerful affirmation and absorb it into your system. You will start to notice immeasurable opportunities that will enable you to acquire all the riches you desire.

Focus and go for it

Your golden key to success lies in your capacity to believe that you will succeed. Hold onto this source of *Ultimate Power*; believe, strongly believe. Whatever your consciousness can conceive and believe, you can achieve.

Cultivate the habit of focusing on a single objective at a time, and try not to spread your efforts over many fields and endeavours. Concentrate on one thing at a time, and you will acquire the valuable asset of dependable memory.

When faced with failure, concentrate on looking for the cause, face the facts honestly and take action to avoid repetition of the cause. Don't look for someone to blame for the mistakes. Take responsibility and don't look for excuses or create alibis as an escape route.

Remember, there are no limitations except the ones you set up in your own consciousness. Focus on overcoming your challenges and nothing will stop you from reaching the top. *Focus and go for it, now!*

You are now unstoppable

You have now received the *ultimate key* to become better acquainted with yourself. This is *raw, potent power* within your consciousness which you are able to develop with the *powerful* message in this book. You must now depend on yourself and find your way out of any unpleasant or unfortunate circumstances. You must now close your consciousness to everything that causes you anxiety, fear, anger, pain, envy, greed, jealousy, unnecessary attachments and the desire to get something for nothing.

You are now in a privileged position. You possess within your consciousness the sacred *Ultimate Power* to succeed. You should by now discover your true self – that other self who makes use of every experience of life. Success is now yours, no matter who you are or what may have been the nature and scope of your past failure. You can start succeeding again, now!

Whatever your profession or line of work; whether you are in business for yourself, a company executive, salesperson, clerk, civil servant, secretary, carpenter, bricklayer, shop assistant, lawyer, accountant, school teacher, pilot or scientist – harness and utilise the *Ultimate Creative Power* within your consciousness and the world will beat a path to your door lift you up, recognise you, and reward you accordingly.

The only way is up. Focus and *go for it. You are now unstoppable.* Don't forget that you possess the *Ultimate Creative Power within your consciousness to achieve anything.*

May the Blessings of the Almighty Creator be.

The Only Way is Up

Triumph Notes

PROGRESS • ACHIEVEMENT • SUCCESS

Cut Your Own Firewood

Challenge Notes
PLANS • TARGETS • HOPES